origin story

Mary Burritt Christiansen Poetry Series

Hilda Raz, Series Editor

The Mary Burritt Christiansen Poetry Series publishes two to four books a year that engage and give voice to the realities of living, working, and experiencing the West and the Border as places and as metaphors. The purpose of the series is to expand access to, and the audience for, quality poetry, both single volumes and anthologies, that can be used for general reading as well as in classrooms.

Also available in the Mary Burritt Christiansen Poetry Series:

Nowhere: Poems by Katie Schmid
Ancestral Demon of a Grieving Bride: Poems by Sy Hoahwah
The Definition of Empty: Poems by Bill O'Neill
Feel Puma: Poems by Ray Gonzalez
Grief Land: Poems by Carrie Shipers
The Shadowgraph: Poems by James Cihlar
Crosscut: Poems by Sean Prentiss
The Music of Her Rivers: Poems by Renny Golden
to cleave: poems by Barbara Rockman
After Party: Poems by Noah Blaustein

For additional titles in the Mary Burritt Christiansen Poetry Series, please visit unmpress.com.

origin story   *poems*

gary jackson

University of New Mexico Press   Albuquerque

ISBN 978-0-8263-6301-5 (paper)
ISBN 978-0-8263-6302-2 (e-book)

Library of Congress Control Number: 2021937802

Founded in 1889, the University of New Mexico sits on the traditional homelands of the Pueblo of Sandia. The original peoples of New Mexico Pueblo, Navajo, and Apache since time immemorial have deep connections to the land and have made significant contributions to the broader community statewide. We honor the land itself and those who remain stewards of this land throughout the generations and also acknowledge our committed relationship to Indigenous peoples. We gratefully recognize our history.

Cover photographs courtesy of the author
Designed by Mindy Basinger Hill
Composed in 10.25/14 pt Minion Pro and Metallophile Sp8

for Kim

they want me to remember
their memories
and I keep on remembering
mine
—*Lucille Clifton*

Help me baby, ain't no stranger.
—*The Rolling Stones*

Contents

III

IV

V

A Note on "Interview featuring . . ." Poems

In 2010, my mother invited me to record a series of conversations with her while we combed through old photos together. The original intention was to use the conversations as inspiration for some future series of poems. Years later, all thirteen of our recorded conversations were transcribed, generating a sixty-page document that was subsequently transformed into the "Interview featuring . . ." erasure poems in this collection.

The following guidelines were used:

1. Each poem is based on a separate conversation.
2. Only two speakers are present in each interview: my mother and myself. My voice is always italicized.
3. When my mother quotes someone else, her voice is also italicized.
4. The grammar and syntax of our conversations could not be "corrected." We talk how we talk.
5. Erasures were guided by an effort to preserve clarity and the music of my mother's voice.
6. Spacing was manipulated to condense what would otherwise amount to massive amounts of white space between words. Caesuras and line endings may signal an omission of just one word, or pages of text.

holoprosencephaly (hŏl'ō-prŏs'ĕn-sĕf'ə-lē)

noun

1. because I never understood: I called it down-syndrome / handicap / retarded / disease that destroys the brain / the body before it has a chance to fall into this world: wet & cold days, waiting on the bus and its long mechanical tongue rolling toward us: me in my mittens, my sister in her wheelchair, our mother behind us both, pushing us toward its teeth, not out of cruelty, but because all children are eventually swallowed: tomorrow I'll be the stupid boy holding a bag of chips out to the boy with one eye on his forehead, the other brown like mine: he sees right through me, knows that I'm afraid: my mother hits me upside the head and demands I share in this waiting while my sister / her daughter is held down on a table, racked by machines & needles to determine why she is still alive: this was supposed to be a definition poem, but I'd rather define the shape of my ignorance / my mother's loss / my own silent betrayal when years later, out of nowhere, my mother said *I never meant for us to grow up so fast*: apologizing for the simple fact we were alive: I forgot my tongue: I want back the years when my mother, younger than I am now, raising two children, would sometimes burst into song: *I am immortal, I have inside me blood of kings!* made me a believer that be it flood or fire, hurricane or heart attack, gunshot or simply the body giving itself back to dust, we could never die: save slowly, until there was only one of us left

The Body You Remember

Consider how it recalls the simplest movements.
How it always shoots the right foot first.
It never forgets where to hold tight the apex

of a cursive G before rounding her sloping curve.
The body never betrays.
But how many times have you

confused *anticipate* with *expect*,
forgotten the names of novels
you read, left your keys

in the door, lost your father's
birthday, your best friend's last name?
Memories flake like dead skin,

carpet the hardwood floors.
Your last birthday settling
over your first fight in sixth grade.

No, the body doesn't betray. Years of use
never dulls memory's blade. Every action
embedded through muscle into bone.

It's still able to unlock every act,
even if you've forgotten how.

Cry Uncle

The Strangest Man of All Time!!
Fantasy as you like it!
Is he Man or Monster or is he both?
—*Incredible Hulk* #1 (1962)

Thirteen & thinking he's on his way
to becoming a man, my cousin
barks *fuck you* to his father,
who only looks at him before

dragging him outside
& raising both fists. Wanting
to speak the same language,
my cousin balls his hands

& his father beats him
until both of them are slippery
with sweat. Until my cousin
breaks into Camel Blue smoke

& crumples on the front lawn
like his father months later
on the sofa, after clutching
his heart & reaching out

to the boy who can only call
the ambulance & wait
for them to arrive &
zip the body into a bag.

Now we're filtered in black,
standing in the cemetery—
all of us still new to burying
kin. When we shake,

my cousin's hand is full
of heat; he can't stand
to look at us or his father's
body, because back then

we knew men only through
stories instead of breath or
touch or trembling hands.

Graduation

My thighs are sore from the mechanical
bull I was forced to ride for photo-op
for aunts & uncles, cousins too young

to recall the meal, the gaudy décor,
my *YEEEEHAW* as all the white girls applaud
before they're back to serving drinks,

clearing plates with bits of bone & taking
the check my mother's new man pays
with a few bills, making nice with family

he's only just met. I trade a smile
with my mother across the table—
surprised at my loneliness

without her. The sun sings through Tanqueray
half-empty back at my apartment.
Her man says *straight* & we step

onto the rotting balcony & clink.
It's not a competition, but he tells her
he puts it down. She replies

he gets it honest—a little proud,
a little hurt. I pour another drink.
Years from now she'll tell me how

he got locked up & the things
he did when the liquor
got to feeling too good—

if I'd known, I would've tried
to put my hands on him. Instead,
I'm shamed by how mothers

always protect their sons. *You*
a booksmart nigga, he says
on the balcony. *You'll get far.*

We toast. My mother nods,
all smiles with no glass. I pour
another drink to celebrate.

Storyteller

My grandfather laughs when I ask him the name of the bar he took my mother to when she was a baby. *All of 'em.* He doesn't tell me about the '65 Mustang—how he wrecked it while driving drunk down Topeka Blvd.— how my mother, no older than three, flew out the window and the cops found her in a field. *I got a scar just like yours*, my mother shows me. In DC, my grandmother shows me a photo of her fourth husband, who died while visiting home in China. *I keep your photos in a drawer somewhere close*, she says when I ask why there are no photos of us on her walls. My mother calls from Dallas, says my father wants a book about him. *Now why would you want that?* she asks but mails my book to LA anyway. My grandfather says we should all visit my grandmother—but never will. My grandmother laughs: *He's still in Kansas? Good.* My mother never talks to her sisters, feels they are ashamed of her hue. *I came out of the same fucking pussy they came out of*, she says. *Write a poem about that.* The Mustang was repoed, I'm told, because he couldn't keep up on payments. *Bullshit*, my mother says, *you stick with my story, it's better.*

Edith Keeler Must Die!

Remember Joan Collins, boy? Remember
her soft-lighted face when she first meets Kirk

and Spock and how we knew everything
to follow? I gave you worlds in old reruns.

Forgive me,
but I wanted the company.

≈

Those were the years your sister outlived herself:

an alternate world where she should have never
made it outside the globe of my belly.

Cleft newborn —
Her lip is broken, you said. I said

your job, then, would be to keep her
from breaking.

≈

I wanted to believe in the multiverse, that the edge
of forever is a door we could tumble through:

the averted future
when every time I see you, I'm reminded she's gone.

But I promise you, boy, I promise
I won't hate us for it.

≈

Coming home late from work, I told you
to watch over her. I opened

the front door, saw my own body:
mirrors in mirrors

leading to my daughter asleep:
my son the hard shell

coiled around: you
saw me enter. Saw me break into light.

Dear Kimberly (1970)

You would be better off with a woman.
Men will only break your heart—the celestial body

turned debris. Men want to touch every
star. Your father disappears in our bed,

apparition of night, haunting others, I know.
I'll take a ghost over nothing. I fear

you will make the same mistakes.
Your sisters will not worry—

the right man will treat a Korean woman
well. But you are too dark, too pretty,

too young, too much your father's daughter.
You want the man strong as gin,

honest as the bottle is clear.

Pub Crawl

Topeka, Kansas, 1963

Under the half-hung sign—
one nail strong enough to hold
the weight of pressed tin—my
grandfather enters. No money
for babysitting, he cradles
his daughter like a charm
for good luck. She's greeted
with *cutie pies* loud as pool balls
clacking the hard edges

of themselves. Always one drink
ahead, he stumbles through
the door before the next
day catches up to them. Before
the men become glass
shards, full of sharp and
brilliant edges, each face
reflecting cities of light and dark.
Though he wants to ascend
he knows he'll plummet
further, faster—years from now
glass will slice open his vein as
he tumbles to recover the bottle
of sloe gin slipping
from his grasp. She grasps

his hand a little tighter, too young
to touch the heavy in every smile.
She's a new word, the first good
thing he's done. But now it's last
call, he's stayed too long, she's
reaching for his arm, neon
catching her copper hands.

튀기 (Twigi)

Not every mulatto is created
equal. Some get heckled
on subway cars, lynched,
or celebrated in tickertape
parades. My mother can't speak

a lick of Korean and doesn't
give a damn, never says mulatto
but calls both of us mutts,
though I can't pass for shit but Black:
ask the audience as I stroll in

late. We could use a Hines Ward
to show us the way—tell the boys
shouting *twigi* on the subway
all of us are animals, are hybrid

of body / of place. Mornings
I dream of kinked hair and cry.
My mother's mother forgets
who we are, speaks Korean
over our heads, lost in language,

my mother only nods. I know
few words, my tongue full
of friction. *Say omma*. Raise us

back into memory, into word,
into place. Once a woman

pressed into the pink nailbeds
of my fingers, said she could see
my blood, my mother

mistaken for Hawaiian,
for Indian, for everything

but what she is. When I say
I'll have no children, she says
I guess we'll be the only

two left. Somewhere
we are understood.
My mother opens her mouth.

Interview featuring girl in hanbok

I didn't like a lotta shit going on. you know,

daddy   was an alcoholic

                    all his buddies still remember me

'cause I be in the joints while he was drinking
shooting craps or whatever they doing

        daddy   just wanna   boy

all them   Korean costumes   are boys' costumes in them pictures.

        Like hanbuk . . . hanbok?

yeah, that's them   the one with the peak
them's boys clothes

                    mama wanted a boy

but   the psychic told her   *if*

    you carry   a boy   your husband will die
dad almost drowned   in Korea

                    mama always   like them psychics

Interview featuring america & three daughters

then   the truth

          What's the truth?

          telling me some shit I already know

          What do you mean?

mama   told everybody   I was the only baby she had

          I stayed there almost a year

          Stayed where?

in Korea   we come here to the States

          and mom   didn't like it   after she see

hairdressers   only do white folks' hair

     they don't understand until they see   firsthand

          that friend mama had   left her Black

and started a new family with   white

          she told daddy   she wanted to go back

and that's how grandma kept me   they left

How long were they there?

probably a year
dad adopted Siri

Siri always was mad at mama said *you kept Kimberly and y'all*

just threw me away

the other daughter didn't want to come

mama
  a couple years ago thought she was gonna die

she told me the truth and I said well mama

I already knew Siri was my sister

grandma told me when I was little

Why did she tell you?

it was the truth!

grandma ain't dumb

        funny

   Siri came   the other   didn't

     I wonder if   there are pictures of

her and   me

Interview featuring boy in wheelchair

Siri   liked them white boys
   daddy   would take   vacuum-cleaner hoses and hit her

mama   picked up a glass ashtray and threw it at me

                                                    I was
bad   I admit that

I would   put

mama's bra over my clothes and be outside playing and dancing
people go by just laughing because I was real little

I remember this other girl

we'd go up and down the street   and beg for candy

her brother   would try to mess with me   but he couldn't do
     much   he had a broken leg

     You mean he broke it, or it was perpetually broken?

he was in a wheelchair   always trying to feel on me
                               I wasn't nothing but seven then

     How old was he?

he was a teenager

     Ah shit.

           see   a lot of stuff could've happened to me
that's why I   liked to stay with grandma

           we just   attached to one another
know what I mean   she was a hard woman

        I remember some   things   real good

you try not to remember shit
                but   I   remember

II

Shazam

I can be onyx under starless sky. I roll
out of bed. I can be hot night

when even talking makes a body sweat.
I can be smog-streaked window,
dirty reflection. Seoul welcomes me

like any stranger. I can be neon: holy cross
outlined in red, love motel pink
shining brighter. I can be lightning,

can be boy, can be man,
be shadow. Tonight
I want to walk, be a bottle

half-drunk, chipped glass, another round.
Be doorman to darkness

because any metropolis wears me down
over time. I can be
your shot of bourbon, your favorite

superhero; let me be
foreigner, your favorite kin, thin
machinery worn to good use.

I can be weapon, be sand,
can *be camera*, be *black-eyed
aperture*, be polite, be empty

bottle, be a wreck of a man
when I put my mind to it.
When I don't.

Café Americano

Quick, catch a last glance at the woman
who spies you at the café, a question
mark that pulls you away
from your work. You feel she's caught
on what strange noun your body is / is not.

Earlier, a young man stood at your
table, waited as you slid off your head-
phones. He asked in Korean if you spoke
English, you said yes, he said maybe
you could teach him how to speak.
You taught him excuses, he still offered

his card. But now the woman hooks
your neurosis: how American do you / do you
not look? Every time a pupil rolls your way,
you think of the children and how

they laughed when they saw you through
the café window. Pointing and shouting,
they knocked each other upside the head
just to get a look at you, laughing
/ laughing.

You wanted to be a mirror, to point back,
to marvel at their strange. In Tokyo,
you caught yourself speaking Korean
to Japanese strangers. They rolled with it.
Maybe you should too. When you get up

to leave, pack your things, you don't notice
how she smiles at you, wants to wave hello /
good-bye. Instead you down dregs of coffee
that leave grounds on your tongue. Roll
them on the inside of your teeth.

Honey

Leaning against the car door, heavy
with whiskey-breath, you ask if this
will last. I'd like to believe

in the power of the word —
all it takes is a voice to etch fire onto stone.
The right words salve bodies, conjure

form from smoke — wisps of curve
solid as charcoal. But we're just
air pushing and pulling

between two mouths. Is it
any wonder why
we talk like this? Always goading
each other into soothsaying, pouring

so much honey down our throats, sticky
with promises we'll come clean, even when we're aware
of the bloated silence before saying
yes.

Runaway

Thumb jut out—slicing
shadow on the two-lane highway—
when three cars fly by, and I wish
I could outrun every goddamn one.

I'm about to throw in the towel
when a cobalt-blue Mercedes pulls
over. Two gorgeous women roll
down the window and ask where
I'm going. *Anywhere but here*
I always reply and they always smile—

but it's when I get in the back seat,
cold air blasting from all sides,
that I miss the desert heat.
They race 95 down Route 54:

on their way to Lubbock, they say,
though they're going the wrong way.
I'm thankful for the break, but wish I could

sit in front, see the road
as we face it head-on,
instead of catching the rust-
colored landscape gallop past.

The redhead turns and asks—
her breath full of coffee and wet metal—
Hey, don't I know you from somewhere?

Like everything,
it's a perfect lie. We'll never get
where we're going. The desert
evening cools us into dream.

Itaewon

At night, the district neons. Syncopated
bass pounces out of buildings,
claiming foreigners. Women
call you into basement bars
rimmed with American whiskey
triple the price: you pay
for the company you keep.
Everyone's plastered & thin
as beer labels, peeled
& wet, papering the floor.
Blink & you'll lose her
for another blue-eyed
military man with thick arms,
a Cubs baseball cap, young
& away from home, eager
for anything Asian. The streets
are lined with Nigerian & Turkish
men hustling toys & jewelry
on cardboard showrooms,
blasting dance hall from boomboxes,
trying their best to blend
into the airwaves. The subway
won't open for another three hours,
so you pop in fog-filled clubs,
hoping crunk will keep your eyes
open, your mouth wet with hunger.

The Body's Language

Men smoke and loiter on Hagwon-Ga, eyeing
the dark borders of my body.

Silence is its own language. Say nothing
and understand the body's meaning.

A grandma gestures to a granddaughter
a command to greet a stranger,

I catch on quick: *Anyang*—the word tastes
hot as it leaves my mouth. I lack grace

of tongue, but become expert at mime—
an open menu, shape of fruit, fingers sign

money, costs, lost places, here and there.
But I understand stares

and gestures, eyes and voices in low
tones. I pretend I don't want to know.

On the subway, halmeoni places her girl
in my arms. Her body becomes word.

Dear Kimberly (1962)

My brothers split wealth, told me
my hands were never big enough,
arms not strong enough to hold
my own fortune. So during Chuseok
I dressed you in baji to fool
the spirits. Prayed for boys bringing coins,

silver and slender as the waning
moon. Most nights I don't dream

of their half-drawn faces, don't lament
the old world we left behind. But I want
your name golden, you beyond
every man's reach; I want blood
to matter. I want America to be
the promise that finally came through.

Fugue with One Voice Longing for Company

It's raining in Anyang. Cherry
blossoms splatter pavement,
subways pulse through

underground arteries, twin
towers rise from the sky,
reminding me of home—its absence,

smog thick like mascara, wet and rolling
down the outlines of buildings.
I inhale, cough, spit like the old

women who dart off buses
across slick streets, dying
to get home.

Anodyne

Bourbon in hand, you believe the world
will always be this strange
and wonderful. A dog barks by the pool
tables; you throw one thigh across my lap
and let your glass draw your hand against mine.
The dark honey crashes against the rim.
A waitress comes and asks if we'd like more.
We nod and raise our down
-ed glasses before drowning. Want burns
our throats. The only thing to cool this is
to spit in my mouth before we smolder back
to clay. Outside, music dies as it stumbles
out of the club. Let us celebrate
how distant our bodies are from home,
how anything can be exotic: the street-view
window, the cracked glass tabletops, our
own skin. Let tonight end somewhere in
foreign territory. Help me believe the lie:
that the world is too vast to ever be familiar.

Interview featuring sisters

all mama's husbands   died except dad

and that's the one she left
     a psychic told her if she stayed   he would die

     Why'd you stay with grandma?

I didn't like staying with them
     grandma said she didn't want

to give me back   said *if you take Kimberly*   *I'll die*

     Siri   *stayed with them?*

sometimes

     I   remember when Siri and I went trick-or-treating one year

remember that slab in the back
     remember she put S-I-R-I   when it was still wet

     So y'all got along, huh?

     yeah   we come up together

III

Seoul

≋

Good soju is smooth like water, unlike
makgeolli, unfiltered, with more color—
feels stranger on my tongue, like communion,
like grandmother meeting her first (?) husband
at a makgeolli bar, their brief union
produced my blood: made in the motherland.

~

Makgeolli is fermented rice, leaves snow
in my mouth. Soju stings like cold metal.
During Hweshik I learn to toast and throw
shots on hardwood floors, leaving wet petals
of liquor to be wiped clean by waiters.
More tradition that makes me feel traitor—
blackout drunk and wondering how it is
I'm standing in the park with two women—
vomiting among the bushes and trees.

≈

Both drinks are cheap, but makgeolli is eight-
percent alcohol, soju is twenty:
similar to my ethnic real estate.
What's the going rate for Black blood / Korean?

≈

The bartender pours free shots for my friends.
She rounds up five random Americans.

≈

Smiling women holding bottles of green:
Be White! blazons an ad, ignore the pang
of hate; sometimes it's better to be seen,
like when the drunk woman ran her finger
down my arm, awed by her still-clean digits.
Untraceable, she tries to say, but slurs.

~

Makgeolli is a drink made for vignettes.
Meant for sipping, some prefer it ice-cold
from a glass, or warm and ladled to hold
the sweetness with heat. It's better homemade,
some say, to ferment in an earthen jar,
buried like grandmother's kimchi in clay
pots in the States—the uprooted backyard.
Godawful, my mother recalls the smell.
I joke how she should miss food from her home.
I ain't there now, she says. I feel compelled,
years later, to try the foods she disowned.

～

Remember to shake or stir makgeolli
before drinking, or the spirit divides.
Fellow expats take note and say to me
these are your people. My class then decides
to teach me *pyongshin* if I teach them *ass-
hole*. Someone jokes that I could always pass.

Interview featuring gun & three daddies

you not supposed to give babies honey

we stayed down there a good while   but after
        they tried to kill   I said I ain't gonna be able to do it

            Wait, but   *I was born in Kansas, right?*

yup

        I got pregnant   on my birthday

    you was nine months later

                        always said mama's baby   daddy's maybe

            That was the last time I saw him?

no

        Oh,   *yeah,*   *LA.*

                that's when   he said *get in the car*
                he said   *get in the car*

                I didn't know what the hell was going on
                            I didn't see the gun

ya grandma Beverly had a hard life
                    she seen her mother get killed
                    her   daddy   was real light

        Carl's daddy
                                        was a Jackson

he was a whatchacall them   a bigamy   bigamy

        Polygamist?

polygamy whatever

so Beverly gave Carl that name too see   that's just like us   we all like that

            separated   divorced

    married   pregnant

                            adopted

you know   I
        just laugh

(Laughter)

                that's how we came up

Interview featuring marriage advice

                         mama   say

               this is what I want you to say

I'm looking for an American man   a tall man

his retirement   like six thousand a month

                                               an   old

man   to get me the keys to his   nice house

                       a good churchgoing   man

                         that would   pass   and leave

everything
            but the man

Interview featuring highway
& two high yellow boys

one cousin   would say
                you was a little yellow boy   what happened?

(Laughter)

      Got dark

(Laughter)

      Is this me when I was born?

yeah   Stuart was born at six-something   Donna and I was in there
together
I walked down the hall to see how she was doing

            you didn't want to come out   Grandma said
      they cut you from end to end   they couldn't cut me no
wider

that's   Carl's sister   your aunt

      she put you in that walker and I said *he can't walk*
you was all over that house   her boy died
             got killed   walking across the highway

IV

Run

The title is a lie: when I tell my wife I'm going for a run what I mean is that I'm going to walk under the hot South Carolina sun for only ten minutes, followed by a minute of actual running, then another ten minutes of walking, then more running, but mostly walking, and by now the sweat has formed a Rorschach mark on my chest and I hate it. Summers, I imagine the better me: the one who runs every morning, who writes all afternoon, who waits until evening to have his first drink. When I say I'm going to write, what I mean is that I'm not going to idle hours browsing blogs, cruising pornography while telling myself it's all in service of the poem I'll one day write on Mia Khalifa and how she was once ranked the #1 porn star in the country and received heaps of hate mail and death threats because she is Lebanese, and I'll call this all research, but I won't know what, exactly, to do with this, or how to put it in a poem, and I forgot to take that run. The run! I will kiss my wife and tell her if I'm not back in forty minutes, come look for me. A joke, when what I mean to say is that it will all be fine, except when the sun begins to set, and a car drives by a little too fast and too close, and my legs tell me my time is up. And now I hate the run, the street, the town, myself, the whole fucking state, and this country for making me feel this way every day I run.

Homecoming

I'm searching the used section. November
whips another flyer in the window
advertising Another Average Brass Band
playing at The Granada. A couple hurries inside
jacketed in leather, collars flipped up;
the bookish clerk mumbles hello
& everything feels like the season

has never changed. I pick up Camus,
a to-do list falls on dust & pine,
demanding: *potatoes & salt,*
dry-cleaned clothes, a paper
on Sisyphus, sex with Ryan.
The sun goes down right
on time. I smile too long

as the clerk gives me my change
& bags the beat-up copy of *The Death*
of Captain Marvel. Outside, the cold
slides a knife in my bones
& wakes me like it should
any creature. *Get used to it,*
I hiss between teeth, bite the frost
from my lip. If I could I'd devour
the winter. Every season, every
prairie & flint hill, every star
& leaping synapse demanding

remember the dog's stupid look,
the countless phone calls,
my friend gone somewhere
I ~~can't~~ won't yet follow,
the service studded with strangers
wondering why I'm not there,
but shit—I'm here now, ain't I?
With another day to kill, another bar to hit
before heading out tomorrow,
this comic my only souvenir.

The Restoration

We drank coffee and got ready,
listened to 93.3 during our commute

to take our mind off how
every day we die on TV. Every day

down the block, kids in surgical masks
spray-paint *Magneto Was Right* on street signs

and new storefronts waiting to redeem
spa-resort passes and avocado-toast dreams

until they, too, are forced out of business.
Or not. Motherfuckers can surprise you,

like beating cancer or criminal charges,
the 2016 election, the high cost

of middle-shelf liquor with a decent view.
If you want to succeed, let them see you

coming, our mothers once said before asking
if we wanted the switch or the belt.

But an ass-whooping beats sitting
at the rooftop bar looking over the steepled skyline

and feeling the pang of worlds we'd rather be,
with two empty seats right beside us

that stay empty for the next two hours,
surrounded by people drinking & eating

standing up—the wind threatening
to blow their hats off their sunburned heads.

Somewhere right now
there are two people looking for those seats.

We keep hoping they'll find them—
find us. Let's have another drink,

watch the muted news above
a row of decent bourbon,

wait to hear, to see
if they make it to us or turn up on TV.

Ode working twice as hard
for fathers and Johnnie Walker

I drank that blue a while back, but I give you
some black, give you some gold,

while my mother, bored, says
show me some poems. So I show her
some poems; hand you the bottle.

Thank you, son. You keep calling me
a word that sounds foreign

from any man talking to me. You talking
about weather? Complaining about rain,
saying *the sun don't like me today.*

My father still calls my mother. You say,
That nigga wants his family back

and we laugh it off. But you fast asleep
beside her, when my father asks,
his voice full of gin and static, *Why*

doesn't he call me back?
After so many years there are two men
who want to fill the same space.

Drunk, you confess some nights you dream
yourself on fire and wake up howling.

You need Jesus, my mother says. You look at her,
thinking of the baby she lost, how you cried.
Wanting to relieve your pain, she told you,

It's better this way: since you ain't
working, I'd have to choose who to keep.

You wanted to argue, but she's done it before.
She's laughing now, reading lines from a poem:
You want a man strong as gin—what you think

that means? She knows the answer.
Shit, I don't know? Now you wondering

if you failing another test. I'd chime in
but I'm busy thinking 'bout the red I still have:
should've given you that. And took that gold back.

Watch

tonight my mother calls
                        you better keep a watch out
                in your city

I remind her *I don't go to church   so you knew*

    I was safe

you need to stop
        she reminds me of fear
older than me

                that if given the chance
    to argue   for my own right   to live
I could still be denied
                                we drove cross-country

        in a U-Haul & a car

        & when the cop pulled each of us
                        over   he asked the same questions

where are you going
what do you do for a living   & when my mother told him
                                her son was a professor
you must be proud

        it took a week to calm her down   as if being
                        calm
    helped anything

                        tomorrow I will try to teach
poets they should bear witness

                                              to the world
                              they walk through

              but we all hesitate
to confront so much white space
                                                  tomorrow

              my wife will sob in her sleep
& wake up & grab me & when

        I ask if she had a bad dream   she will say   *yes*

there are two women   in my life
                  who will always
fear
                  what happens to my body &

      this awareness makes me   more aware
of my own body

      than I have ever been
& there's no
                  way to communicate this
                                          to you
        who are not in this body

        you just
                  have to trust

        when I say   it's exhausting

work
        to keep a watch out in my city

                                  to keep watch
in every city
              we have ever lived

Star Trek VI

Listen, Dad called the other day about my reading in
LA, said he couldn't make it since he was going back
in, but told me I should visit my sister. *She's been dying*

to see you her whole life. Over drinks, my mother
shows me photo albums to glimpse a trace
of Dad's second family, of the girl I'll meet,

the man he eventually became / always was.
Mom pours her cognac into my glass; when she
watches me down what's left, she sees my father

and some days this worries her. But this poem
ain't his. This poem belongs in the maroon café in LA.

My big bro is a professor. She doesn't mean any
harm, only wants to see a little blood over coffee.
You have Dad's eyes, she says, *and his nose.* I touch

the undiscovered country of his face. Each of us
struggles to become what the other conjures,
take pictures I've since lost. *Call me sometime bro,*

as if saying a thing makes it true. Some words
I haven't been in twenty years. You know me,
I'm better at being a brother to ghosts.

After the Reading

a woman walked up and asked how

the young Black poet the month before
could shake with such anger during

his reading. Is it really
that bad? It can't be that bad,
can it?

I told her it was
and she said,

Maybe for you

in Kansas, but here in Charleston
a nice Black man held the door open
for me and my friends
because people respect each other here
and those things you write about
don't happen anymore.

I live here, too, I reminded her.
And by here I meant the world,

but she was already off and talking
about some professor that was

B-L-A-C-K Black,
not Black like you,
and when I was in college in the '70s,
I couldn't understand why on earth
he would come here to teach
in a state where people just don't see
that kind of Black.

The woman serving wine at the reception
exchanged a look with me—
each of us with arched brows
asking the other,
You believe this shit?

Then another woman
tried to help, said,

It doesn't matter what color anyone is
as long as you're willing to listen
to one another's experience—
but those young people who identify
as different genders are beyond me.

I must have been in a goddamn sitcom
when yet another well-meaning woman
realized they were all starting to look bad
and tried to shut the whole thing down:

Let's talk about the art on the walls,
how good it is to host such a diverse
lineup of poets, how everything's
always been this awful,

but it's getting. Isn't it
getting better?

Alexandria

Boxcars, scotch, cheap bourbon on rocks,
nothing neat: we steady

chasing love from ghosts
over drinks half-slung. Last night
your sister offered us money

for making the long trip to visit,
then the two of you quizzed your mother
on the names of the living & the dead &

corrected every wrong answer.

She kept calling me your husband
instead of your son. How can family be stranger
the closer we become? We ain't

slurring yet, but well on our way
when you ask do I remember your sister's name

scrawled in concrete in the backyard:
Siri was here—1968,
& how the yard & the slab & the house

got up & left us one day & if you had more time
you would've burned the whole fucking city down.

You got me here so you wouldn't be lonely,
so one day I could conjure
your mother's voice—my one good trick.

It's been forty years since you spoke

mother, sister, last
round, let's swap

another story in this shit
Virginia bar without a single-
malt scotch. Grab a few tall boys

for the nursing home: your mother's
lonely, your sister's on her way.

Interview featuring white boy

where's that one boy I used to throw rocks with?
he's probably gone

     You used to throw rocks with or at?

with   he's a bad white boy

Interview featuring sister

That ain't our house.

> yeah   that's our house
> we put that thing on the couch
>
> that's the water bed

That damn bed.

> I was   pregnant with Gina
> then

You didn't want to get pregnant again, did you?

> uh-uh

I don't blame you.

> there's you and grandma

That's Easter or something, you got that hat on!

> mmm-hmm

Look like you stylin'.

> it was slick

Yeah.

          there's you and Gina
          before she got her lip fixed

With her wild hair.

          she look fat like a butterball
          look at her

Look at you

Why does that happen?

          cleft lip   they say
          that happens a lot in Korea

          they didn't   tell us
          she was gonna be handicapped
          they said
          she got a cleft palette they could fix

          but   you could tell   something
          else was wrong

How come they didn't   ?

grandma knew   could feel   she
didn't have a soft spot
we went to Kansas City   KU medical center

they said she got severe handicaps

They was afraid   .

she was always gonna be a baby   you
could see it

Interview featuring shape-shifting mother

I'm   a lotta people

                              your last year
    a   woulda been

                   the right age

        a dark woman

                    I can't think   I know

when we grin

            there it is   teasing you
                                   AWWWW

        you starting to get   it

                    know what I mean

            hard

                   like   I couldn't understand

               strong

        but

what about

reunion *(?)*

      lord   come

and   change

    my
        picture

make   us

        like that again

V

Kansas

It's love you left, we'll say
when you never come back
for bells for the dead, for the grave-
stone heads: the only ones
that don't keep count. Don't
we know it's love that keeps you
away, that marks every mile
devotion? You would've went
to the end with each one,
made Orpheus turn back.
Would've fell / would've leapt /
would've left. The living is easy
/ the leaving is easy / living
with ghosts; it was easy
to give up your home
to your father, struck
with the same grief
of living, demanding
what are you gonna do
with my mama's house?
Shorn grass & damp dirt:
they'll put me in the middle.
I kick the ground like tires,
feeling dumb without flowers /
tokens / grief / anything
in my hands. *You'll bring me*
back home, won't you? Stamp
it down, as if the flat earth
could answer sometimes this,
too, is love. You left.

Elegy That Was Already Done Before

I'm trying to teach these kids about elegy when one of them asks *how
do you grieve?* Everyone answers: crying, screaming in the crook of your
elbow, trying to muffle your soul when all you doing is making it harder
for the dead to hear what you have to say. Only one student says *drink*. I
put one toe in and ask *what?* He says *Jack Daniels b/c I don't have to think*
and now I'm thinking about ghosts again. Last month I talked to your
mother on the phone. My mother wanted to show her my book but ain't
that like rubbing it in someone's face that one of us is gone and the other
got famous for it? Yet here we are—you still dead, and I'm a fool to think
the last poem was the last one I'd write about you. At parties, people who
don't know that too much ash sours the soil ask about you. I bury two
fingers in my temple—one fingernail buried under skin, the other not far
behind. Everything is about loss. About stories, about superheroes, about
trying to show these motherfucking students what an elegy is really about.
It's about the student who asked *who's your favorite superhero?* and I said
Spider-Man when I should have said you.

Creature

I'm turning lighter

    with every cat-scratch-
            made-morse-code—

                high yellow dashes

run down my arms

reminding me of family

reunions when aunties would say *you used to be*

    such a lil' yellow boy.
          What happened?

Summers

women smiled at how dark I could become

when I was young

with a mane of oiled black hair.

But I've always preferred to be

           amnesiac /

to drink / have *time enough at last*

with my books & broken glasses

my television & half-empty bottles

my thinning hair   my growing beard

my gut   my body keeps

compensating for itself—

                    my future's going brighter.

Wait long enough,

maybe they'll let me back in

the club. When my mother turned one

                    she got her first gray hair,
when she turned thirty

she buried her eight-year-old.

Hereditary, she said. I'm still learning

what it means.

Multiple Man:
Guest-starring me & you

Every night I sleep on alternate

sides of the bed, as if to duplicate
sleeping with you. If

I'm fast enough, I'm the warmth
of my own body beside me, reach

out and touch myself. Breach
the blue of my bones, breathe in my own ear.

You left me. Lying here,
I left you to be with me.

Someone asks if your body
was worth trading for mine.

My sin was always pride.
Did you want a man who sleeps

with himself to keep
the bed warm? I need you like the earth

needed the flood after dearth.

Saudade

You keep count of the dead up the coast. Ask me how
it would feel to have a sister who would be thirty by now.
What can I say besides I forget my own age some days,
and this loss comforts me? I turn on the radio. We detour
in Fayetteville so you can visit friends you haven't seen
in years. We ask the phone for directions. We stop by
and you talk about your time in the army, how my father
called you *the baddest bitch at Fort Hood*, and is there
a word? There must be a word
for remembering how happy and how sad you once were,
and how you'll never feel that shade again. When we pull
away, I ask how it felt and you say we all look so old. I say
you all look old, I look just fine, and you laugh. You talk
to the phone to get us out of here, but it can't understand,
so I take it from your hands and speak each word slow.

Dear Siri (1963)

Foolish girl, you wonder why I lie? Why I tell
them you are not mine? You are too young

to understand shame. Every plum has a past.
When you puncture the skin, you don't think

of where it's been, but how it tastes.
If someone has already bitten the fruit, left

the flesh exposed in the sun,
would you still eat?

When you are older you will understand
how to preserve blood.

Reunion

I.

Almost midnight, your sister blooms
into a bruised heart, miming
your father's fists, recalling
how your mother *just stood there*

smoking. It's not heartbreak.
Not yet. Only a teenage girl
after school *using furniture
polish as deodorant. He called*

*me a stupid, country girl.
Said they should have left me
in Korea.* The car straddles
both lanes, you just want

to get home. *Do you understand
why I never called? I didn't
hate you, but you understand.
Do you understand?* Standing

in the Holiday Inn, you hug
the hurtling bones of your sister,
not because you understand,
but because you remember

the stray cat on Halloween,
and how you wanted to keep him—
so you put the cat in the bag,
and your grandmother made

you throw all the candy,
sticky with fur, away. Your
sister took the blame, took
the beating. And you placed

all those years, and the people
inside them, deep into the earth,
and kissed each gravestone,
and haven't eaten a Mary Jane
since.

II.

But it's not heartbreak
until the next day
having breakfast
with your mother
and her nurse and
there's nothing
you can say
to get her
to remember
your name
until you show
the photo
of your father
in uniform
her in her white
gown and she calls
his name
so you call him
and put her
on the phone
and she tells him
she misses him
and when is he
going to come
and take her
away? And what
can he say except
I'm on my way
and when she passes

back the phone
it's back
to soggy pancakes
and stale coffee
and before
he hangs up
your father asks:
your son will write
about us still
right?

my father raises his shirt

tattoos cover his chest,
stomach, nipples, *some
are older than you.*
A bottle & two
glasses of bourbon
between us, a swig left
for me, more for him,
though he doesn't take
his time—shoots it
like a man half-
drunk and longing
for reunion. I don't
know what to say,
save drink another
glass, touch his chest—

[Banana-less, my lover returns home]

Banana-less, my lover returns home.
Her story to tell, but I can tell—like Dorothy
and the phrase someone spouts every goddamn time
        they learn where I'm from—

I'm no longer home.   Kansas isn't here,
though the polluted dust feels like pollen
this time of year
    if I close my mouth and will my pores

        to ignore the burning. We blame
China and the North: our favorite scapegoats.
        We blame the origins of things
        instead of the things themselves.

    Pronounce your mother's name. Tell me
        again the town you're from. Remnants
of light fall on our skin.   Get in trouble with me.
        Have a drink outdoors, let neon

catch the rims of our glasses, hook and pull
            us further from the places we're from.

Arlington

It's spring, it's fiction, it's fact, it's scores of women who left
their homes and families by coercion or force or desperation,

survival or love, and if you squint hard enough
they all feel the same. It's 1961, it's Fort Belvoir, Virginia,

it's built on a plantation, it's Dukie Oh
promising to stay in touch with other Korean brides

while she packs to move to Kansas to live
with her husband's family. It's one seat, it's two foreign

bodies, it's her baby girl in her lap. It's 2018,
it's Arlington, it's the obituary calling her 80,

it's no one knows, it's my mother's loving
her mother's last lie. How she knew the years

could be used against you. Sex. And color too
Dukie realized too late. It's none of us

stepping up when the pastor asks *who wants to share
some of the good times they had?* It's how there's so few

of us left. It's the terrible truth, it's my mother
purchasing her own plot the day her daughter died.

It's one last drink before lift-off, it's the little girl
on her mother's lap, it's my mother

who looks forward, looks back
to a place she'll never return — says *Kansas*

is death. And fuck death. It's a promise
she knows she'll break.

Interview featuring thanksgiving

this is just   graduation

you know my name

                you know we go

   I didn't really know

         another time

when the   living   don't   leave

we   remove it

               cut it off

cut it off

             grow   apart

   I think about   them

it's too bad they didn't get to live to see

     who has?

you

           me

Notes

holoprosencephaly (hŏl'ō-prŏs'ĕn-sĕf'ə-lē)
> The italicized song lyrics are from Queen's "Princes of the Universe,"
> which was written for the 1986 film *Highlander*.

Edith Keeler Must Die!
> The poem's title is a direct quote from the 1967 *Star Trek* episode,
> "The City on the Edge of Forever."

튀기 (Twigi)
> Roughly translated from Korean, *twigi* is a derogatory term that means
> "mixed-blood" or "animal hybrid." Hines Ward, who played for the
> Pittsburgh Steelers, was born in Seoul, South Korea, to a Korean mother
> and a Black father.

Shazam
> The italicized lines are from the poem "Instruction, Final: To Brown Poets
> from Black Girl with Silver Leica" by Nikky Finney.

The Body's Language
> Hagwon-Ga is a street in Anyang, South Korea, known for its high
> concentration of private schools and academies.

Acknowledgments

Many thanks to the editors of the following publications, where the following poems originally appeared, some in different forms and titles.

200 New Mexico Poems: "Anodyne"

32 Poems: "Café Americano"

Academy of American Poets Poem-A-Day: "Kansas," "Multiple Man: Guest-starring me & you," and "The Restoration"

Bennington Review: "holoprosencephaly (hŏl'ō-prŏs'ĕn-sĕf'ə-lē)"

Birmingham Poetry Review: "Arlington"

BorderSenses: "Fugue with One Voice, Longing for Company"

Callaloo: "The Body You Remember"

Crab Orchard Review: "Storyteller" and "Runaway"

From the Fishouse: "Itaewon"

Fugue: "Honey"

Ice on a Hot Stove: A Decade of Converse MFA Poetry: "Graduation" and "Homecoming"

The Laurel Review: "Interview featuring shape-shifting mother" and "Interview featuring sister"

Lumina: "Star Trek VI" and "Edith Keeler Must Die!"

Memorious: "Reunion" and "my father raises his shirt"

The Normal School: "The Body's Language"

Obsidian: "Saudade"

Phoebe: "Dear Siri (1963)" and "Dear Kimberly (1970)"

A Poetry Congeries: "[Banana-less, my lover returns home]," "Seoul," and "Creature"

Prairie Schooner: "Run"

Solstice: "Interview featuring girl in hanbok"

Sugar House Review: "Pub Crawl"

The Sun: "After the Reading"

Third Coast: "Interview featuring korea & lilt perms"

Tuesday; An Art Project: "Elegy That Was Already Done Before"

Transition Magazine: "Shazam"

Waxwing Literary Journal: "Dear Kimberly (1962)," "Twigi," "Alexandria," and "Ode working twice as hard for fathers and Johnnie Walker"
Welcome to the Neighborhood: An Anthology of American Coexistence: "Watch"

A heartfelt thanks to the innumerable people who loaned me their time, wisdom, insight, and abiding patience in shaping these poems over the last decade, including Lisa D. Chavez, Kyle Churney, Jonathan Bohr Heinen, Dana Levin, Juan Morales, and far more than I can hope to say here. Special thanks to Esther Lee, who endured reading these poems countless times and always kept me in check. Gratitude to Toi Derricotte, Cornelius Eady, and everyone at Cave Canem for their support, especially during the early stages of many of these poems. And infinite gratitude to Elise McHugh and Hilda Raz and the University of New Mexico Press for giving this book a home.

For Lisa and her endless support both inside and outside of these pages for over fifteen years. Without her, I'd be a lost man.

And for my family, the living and the dead, and their endless encouragement to write and document these fragments of our lives. For my aunts, uncles, cousins, sisters, fathers, and grandfathers. For my grandmother who's no longer here but made an effort to reconnect toward the end of her life. And especially for you—Kim. For everything. This book is yours as much as it is mine.